Over 8,000 cursive tracing

Learn to Write in Cursive

Handwriting Practice Workbook

- Uppercase Cursive Letters

- Lowercase Cursive Letters

- Cursive Sentence Practice

"Learning to write in cursive is shown to improve brain development in the areas of thinking, language and working memory."

--2013 NYT Article

Adrianne L. Mercury

Trace the letter Aa.

A a   Animal

A A A A A A A A A

A A A A A A A A A

A A A A A A A A A

A A A A A A A A A

A A A A A A A A A

A A A A A A A A A

a a a a a a a a a a

a a a a a a a a a a

a a a a a a a a a a a

a a a a a a a a a a a

a a a a a a a a a a a

Trace the letter Aa.

$\mathscr{A}$ a $\mathscr{A}nalyze$

$\mathscr{A}$ $\mathscr{A}$ $\mathscr{A}$ $\mathscr{A}$ $\mathscr{A}$ $\mathscr{A}$ $\mathscr{A}$ $\mathscr{A}$ $\mathscr{A}$ $\mathscr{A}$

$\mathscr{A}$ $\mathscr{A}$ $\mathscr{A}$ $\mathscr{A}$ $\mathscr{A}$ $\mathscr{A}$ $\mathscr{A}$ $\mathscr{A}$ $\mathscr{A}$ $\mathscr{A}$

$\mathscr{A}$ $\mathscr{A}$ $\mathscr{A}$ $\mathscr{A}$ $\mathscr{A}$ $\mathscr{A}$ $\mathscr{A}$ $\mathscr{A}$ $\mathscr{A}$ $\mathscr{A}$

$\mathscr{A}$ $\mathscr{A}$ $\mathscr{A}$ $\mathscr{A}$ $\mathscr{A}$ $\mathscr{A}$ $\mathscr{A}$ $\mathscr{A}$ $\mathscr{A}$ $\mathscr{A}$

$\mathscr{A}$ $\mathscr{A}$ $\mathscr{A}$ $\mathscr{A}$ $\mathscr{A}$ $\mathscr{A}$ $\mathscr{A}$ $\mathscr{A}$ $\mathscr{A}$ $\mathscr{A}$

$\mathscr{A}$ $\mathscr{A}$ $\mathscr{A}$ $\mathscr{A}$ $\mathscr{A}$ $\mathscr{A}$ $\mathscr{A}$ $\mathscr{A}$ $\mathscr{A}$

a a a a a a a a a a

a a a a a a a a a a

a a a a a a a a a a

a a a a a a a a a a

a a a a a a a a a a

Trace the letter Aa. Then write the letter Aa as many times as possible.

A a Alphabet

a a a

a a a

a a a

a a a

a a a

a a a

a a a

a a a

a a a

a a a

a a a

Learn to Write in Cursive: Handwriting Practice Workbook

Write the sentence onto the lines below. Then trace and write the letters.

A was an ant

Who seldom stood still,

He made a very nice house

In the side of a hill.

a a

A A

a a a

a a a

Trace the letter Bb.

$\mathcal{B}$ $\mathcal{b}$ $\mathcal{Bubble}$

$\mathcal{B}$ $\mathcal{B}$ $\mathcal{B}$ $\mathcal{B}$ $\mathcal{B}$ $\mathcal{B}$ $\mathcal{B}$ $\mathcal{B}$ $\mathcal{B}$ $\mathcal{B}$ $\mathcal{B}$

$\mathcal{B}$ $\mathcal{B}$ $\mathcal{B}$ $\mathcal{B}$ $\mathcal{B}$ $\mathcal{B}$ $\mathcal{B}$ $\mathcal{B}$ $\mathcal{B}$ $\mathcal{B}$ $\mathcal{B}$

$\mathcal{B}$ $\mathcal{B}$ $\mathcal{B}$ $\mathcal{B}$ $\mathcal{B}$ $\mathcal{B}$ $\mathcal{B}$ $\mathcal{B}$ $\mathcal{B}$ $\mathcal{B}$ $\mathcal{B}$

$\mathcal{B}$ $\mathcal{B}$ $\mathcal{B}$ $\mathcal{B}$ $\mathcal{B}$ $\mathcal{B}$ $\mathcal{B}$ $\mathcal{B}$ $\mathcal{B}$ $\mathcal{B}$ $\mathcal{B}$

$\mathcal{B}$ $\mathcal{B}$ $\mathcal{B}$ $\mathcal{B}$ $\mathcal{B}$ $\mathcal{B}$ $\mathcal{B}$ $\mathcal{B}$ $\mathcal{B}$ $\mathcal{B}$ $\mathcal{B}$

$\mathcal{B}$ $\mathcal{B}$ $\mathcal{B}$ $\mathcal{B}$ $\mathcal{B}$ $\mathcal{B}$ $\mathcal{B}$ $\mathcal{B}$ $\mathcal{B}$ $\mathcal{B}$ $\mathcal{B}$

$\mathcal{b}$ $\mathcal{b}$ $\mathcal{b}$ $\mathcal{b}$ $\mathcal{b}$ $\mathcal{b}$ $\mathcal{b}$ $\mathcal{b}$ $\mathcal{b}$

$\mathcal{b}$ $\mathcal{b}$ $\mathcal{b}$ $\mathcal{b}$ $\mathcal{b}$ $\mathcal{b}$ $\mathcal{b}$ $\mathcal{b}$ $\mathcal{b}$

$\mathcal{b}$ $\mathcal{b}$ $\mathcal{b}$ $\mathcal{b}$ $\mathcal{b}$ $\mathcal{b}$ $\mathcal{b}$ $\mathcal{b}$ $\mathcal{b}$

$\mathcal{b}$ $\mathcal{b}$ $\mathcal{b}$ $\mathcal{b}$ $\mathcal{b}$ $\mathcal{b}$ $\mathcal{b}$ $\mathcal{b}$ $\mathcal{b}$

$\mathcal{b}$ $\mathcal{b}$ $\mathcal{b}$ $\mathcal{b}$ $\mathcal{b}$ $\mathcal{b}$ $\mathcal{b}$ $\mathcal{b}$ $\mathcal{b}$

Learn to Write in Cursive: Handwriting Practice Workbook

Trace the letter Bb.

Trace the letter Bb. Then write the letter Bb as many times as possible.

B b Baby

B B B

B B B

B B B

B B B

B B B

B B B

b b b

b b b

b b b

b b b

b b b

Learn to Write in Cursive: Handwriting Practice Workbook

Write the sentence onto the lines below. Then trace and write the letters.

B was a book

With a binding of blue

And pictures and stories

For me and for you.

B B B

B B B

b b b

b b b

Trace the letter Cc.

C c Cackle

C C C C C C C C C C C C C C C C

C C C C C C C C C C C C C C C C

C C C C C C C C C C C C C C C C

C C C C C C C C C C C C C C C C

C C C C C C C C C C C C C C C C

C C C C C C C C C C C C C C C C

c c c c c c c c c c c c c c c c

c c c c c c c c c c c c c c c c

c c c c c c c c c c c c c c c c

c c c c c c c c c c c c c c c c

c c c c c c c c c c c c c c c c

Trace the letter Cc.

Cc Concentrate

$\mathcal{C}$ $\mathcal{C}$ $\mathcal{C}$ $\mathcal{C}$ $\mathcal{C}$ $\mathcal{C}$ $\mathcal{C}$ $\mathcal{C}$ $\mathcal{C}$ $\mathcal{C}$ $\mathcal{C}$ $\mathcal{C}$ $\mathcal{C}$ $\mathcal{C}$

$\mathcal{C}$ $\mathcal{C}$ $\mathcal{C}$ $\mathcal{C}$ $\mathcal{C}$ $\mathcal{C}$ $\mathcal{C}$ $\mathcal{C}$ $\mathcal{C}$ $\mathcal{C}$ $\mathcal{C}$ $\mathcal{C}$ $\mathcal{C}$ $\mathcal{C}$

$\mathcal{C}$ $\mathcal{C}$ $\mathcal{C}$ $\mathcal{C}$ $\mathcal{C}$ $\mathcal{C}$ $\mathcal{C}$ $\mathcal{C}$ $\mathcal{C}$ $\mathcal{C}$ $\mathcal{C}$ $\mathcal{C}$ $\mathcal{C}$ $\mathcal{C}$

$\mathcal{C}$ $\mathcal{C}$ $\mathcal{C}$ $\mathcal{C}$ $\mathcal{C}$ $\mathcal{C}$ $\mathcal{C}$ $\mathcal{C}$ $\mathcal{C}$ $\mathcal{C}$ $\mathcal{C}$ $\mathcal{C}$ $\mathcal{C}$ $\mathcal{C}$

$\mathcal{C}$ $\mathcal{C}$ $\mathcal{C}$ $\mathcal{C}$ $\mathcal{C}$ $\mathcal{C}$ $\mathcal{C}$ $\mathcal{C}$ $\mathcal{C}$ $\mathcal{C}$ $\mathcal{C}$ $\mathcal{C}$ $\mathcal{C}$ $\mathcal{C}$

$\mathcal{C}$ $\mathcal{C}$ $\mathcal{C}$ $\mathcal{C}$ $\mathcal{C}$ $\mathcal{C}$ $\mathcal{C}$ $\mathcal{C}$ $\mathcal{C}$ $\mathcal{C}$ $\mathcal{C}$ $\mathcal{C}$ $\mathcal{C}$ $\mathcal{C}$

c c c c c c c c c c c c c c

c c c c c c c c c c c c c c

c c c c c c c c c c c c c c

c c c c c c c c c c c c c c

c c c c c c c c c c c c c c

Trace the letter Cc. Then write the letter Cc as many times as possible.

$\mathcal{C}$ c   Camel

$\mathcal{C}$ $\mathcal{C}$ $\mathcal{C}$

$\mathcal{C}$ $\mathcal{C}$ $\mathcal{C}$

$\mathcal{C}$ $\mathcal{C}$ $\mathcal{C}$

$\mathcal{C}$ $\mathcal{C}$ $\mathcal{C}$

$\mathcal{C}$ $\mathcal{C}$ $\mathcal{C}$

$\mathcal{C}$ $\mathcal{C}$ $\mathcal{C}$

c c c

c c c

c c c

c c c

c c c

Write the sentence onto the lines below. Then trace and write the letters.

C was a cat

Who ran after a rat

But his courage did fail

When she seized on his tail.

C C C

C C C

c c c

c c c

Trace the letter Dd.

D d Daffodil

D D D D D D D D D D D

D D D D D D D D D D D

D D D D D D D D D D D

D D D D D D D D D D D

D D D D D D D D D D D

D D D D D D D D D D D

d d d d d d d d d d d d d

d d d d d d d d d d d d d

d d d d d d d d d d d d d

d d d d d d d d d d d d d

d d d d d d d d d d d d d

Trace the letter Dd.

$\mathcal{D}$ d $\mathcal{D}estructive$

$\mathcal{D}$ $\mathcal{D}$ $\mathcal{D}$ $\mathcal{D}$ $\mathcal{D}$ $\mathcal{D}$ $\mathcal{D}$ $\mathcal{D}$ $\mathcal{D}$ $\mathcal{D}$

$\mathcal{D}$ $\mathcal{D}$ $\mathcal{D}$ $\mathcal{D}$ $\mathcal{D}$ $\mathcal{D}$ $\mathcal{D}$ $\mathcal{D}$ $\mathcal{D}$ $\mathcal{D}$

$\mathcal{D}$ $\mathcal{D}$ $\mathcal{D}$ $\mathcal{D}$ $\mathcal{D}$ $\mathcal{D}$ $\mathcal{D}$ $\mathcal{D}$ $\mathcal{D}$ $\mathcal{D}$

$\mathcal{D}$ $\mathcal{D}$ $\mathcal{D}$ $\mathcal{D}$ $\mathcal{D}$ $\mathcal{D}$ $\mathcal{D}$ $\mathcal{D}$ $\mathcal{D}$ $\mathcal{D}$

$\mathcal{D}$ $\mathcal{D}$ $\mathcal{D}$ $\mathcal{D}$ $\mathcal{D}$ $\mathcal{D}$ $\mathcal{D}$ $\mathcal{D}$ $\mathcal{D}$ $\mathcal{D}$

$\mathcal{D}$ $\mathcal{D}$ $\mathcal{D}$ $\mathcal{D}$ $\mathcal{D}$ $\mathcal{D}$ $\mathcal{D}$ $\mathcal{D}$ $\mathcal{D}$ $\mathcal{D}$

d d d d d d d d d d d d

d d d d d d d d d d d d

d d d d d d d d d d d d

d d d d d d d d d d d d

d d d d d d d d d d d d

Trace the letter Dd. Then write the letter Dd as many times as possible.

D d Daytime

D D D

D D D

D D D

D D D

D D D

D D D

d d d

d d d

d d d

d d d

d d d

Learn to Write in Cursive: Handwriting Practice Workbook

Write the sentence onto the lines below. Then trace and write the letters.

D was a dove,

Who lived in a wood,

With such pretty soft wings,

And so gentle and good!

D D D

D D D

d d d

d d d

Trace the letter Ee.

$\mathcal{E}$ e $\mathcal{E}$xcite

$\mathcal{E}$ $\mathcal{E}$ $\mathcal{E}$ $\mathcal{E}$ $\mathcal{E}$ $\mathcal{E}$ $\mathcal{E}$ $\mathcal{E}$ $\mathcal{E}$ $\mathcal{E}$ $\mathcal{E}$ $\mathcal{E}$ $\mathcal{E}$ $\mathcal{E}$

$\mathcal{E}$ $\mathcal{E}$ $\mathcal{E}$ $\mathcal{E}$ $\mathcal{E}$ $\mathcal{E}$ $\mathcal{E}$ $\mathcal{E}$ $\mathcal{E}$ $\mathcal{E}$ $\mathcal{E}$ $\mathcal{E}$ $\mathcal{E}$ $\mathcal{E}$

$\mathcal{E}$ $\mathcal{E}$ $\mathcal{E}$ $\mathcal{E}$ $\mathcal{E}$ $\mathcal{E}$ $\mathcal{E}$ $\mathcal{E}$ $\mathcal{E}$ $\mathcal{E}$ $\mathcal{E}$ $\mathcal{E}$ $\mathcal{E}$ $\mathcal{E}$

$\mathcal{E}$ $\mathcal{E}$ $\mathcal{E}$ $\mathcal{E}$ $\mathcal{E}$ $\mathcal{E}$ $\mathcal{E}$ $\mathcal{E}$ $\mathcal{E}$ $\mathcal{E}$ $\mathcal{E}$ $\mathcal{E}$ $\mathcal{E}$ $\mathcal{E}$

$\mathcal{E}$ $\mathcal{E}$ $\mathcal{E}$ $\mathcal{E}$ $\mathcal{E}$ $\mathcal{E}$ $\mathcal{E}$ $\mathcal{E}$ $\mathcal{E}$ $\mathcal{E}$ $\mathcal{E}$ $\mathcal{E}$ $\mathcal{E}$ $\mathcal{E}$

$\mathcal{E}$ $\mathcal{E}$ $\mathcal{E}$ $\mathcal{E}$ $\mathcal{E}$ $\mathcal{E}$ $\mathcal{E}$ $\mathcal{E}$ $\mathcal{E}$ $\mathcal{E}$ $\mathcal{E}$ $\mathcal{E}$ $\mathcal{E}$ $\mathcal{E}$

e e e e e e e e e e e e e e

e e e e e e e e e e e e e e

e e e e e e e e e e e e e e

e e e e e e e e e e e e e e

e e e e e e e e e e e e e e

Trace the letter Ee.

E e Extraordinary

Trace the letter Ee. Then write the letter Ee as many times as possible.

$\mathscr{E}$ $\mathscr{e}$ $\mathscr{Excellent}$

$\mathscr{E}$ $\mathscr{E}$ $\mathscr{E}$

$\mathscr{E}$ $\mathscr{E}$ $\mathscr{E}$

$\mathscr{E}$ $\mathscr{E}$ $\mathscr{E}$

$\mathscr{E}$ $\mathscr{E}$ $\mathscr{E}$

$\mathscr{E}$ $\mathscr{E}$ $\mathscr{E}$

$\mathscr{E}$ $\mathscr{E}$ $\mathscr{E}$

$\mathscr{e}$ $\mathscr{e}$ $\mathscr{e}$

$\mathscr{e}$ $\mathscr{e}$ $\mathscr{e}$

$\mathscr{e}$ $\mathscr{e}$ $\mathscr{e}$

$\mathscr{e}$ $\mathscr{e}$ $\mathscr{e}$

$\mathscr{e}$ $\mathscr{e}$ $\mathscr{e}$

Learn to Write in Cursive: Handwriting Practice Workbook

Write the sentence onto the lines below. Then trace and write the letters.

E was an eagle,

Who sat on the rocks,

And looked down on the

And the far-away flocks.

E E E

E E E

e e e

e e e

Trace the letter Ff.

$\mathcal{F}$ f $\mathcal{F}luffy$

$\mathcal{F}$ $\mathcal{F}$ $\mathcal{F}$ $\mathcal{F}$ $\mathcal{F}$ $\mathcal{F}$ $\mathcal{F}$ $\mathcal{F}$ $\mathcal{F}$ $\mathcal{F}$ $\mathcal{F}$ $\mathcal{F}$ $\mathcal{F}$

$\mathcal{F}$ $\mathcal{F}$ $\mathcal{F}$ $\mathcal{F}$ $\mathcal{F}$ $\mathcal{F}$ $\mathcal{F}$ $\mathcal{F}$ $\mathcal{F}$ $\mathcal{F}$ $\mathcal{F}$ $\mathcal{F}$ $\mathcal{F}$

$\mathcal{F}$ $\mathcal{F}$ $\mathcal{F}$ $\mathcal{F}$ $\mathcal{F}$ $\mathcal{F}$ $\mathcal{F}$ $\mathcal{F}$ $\mathcal{F}$ $\mathcal{F}$ $\mathcal{F}$ $\mathcal{F}$ $\mathcal{F}$

$\mathcal{F}$ $\mathcal{F}$ $\mathcal{F}$ $\mathcal{F}$ $\mathcal{F}$ $\mathcal{F}$ $\mathcal{F}$ $\mathcal{F}$ $\mathcal{F}$ $\mathcal{F}$ $\mathcal{F}$ $\mathcal{F}$ $\mathcal{F}$

$\mathcal{F}$ $\mathcal{F}$ $\mathcal{F}$ $\mathcal{F}$ $\mathcal{F}$ $\mathcal{F}$ $\mathcal{F}$ $\mathcal{F}$ $\mathcal{F}$ $\mathcal{F}$ $\mathcal{F}$ $\mathcal{F}$ $\mathcal{F}$

$\mathcal{F}$ $\mathcal{F}$ $\mathcal{F}$ $\mathcal{F}$ $\mathcal{F}$ $\mathcal{F}$ $\mathcal{F}$ $\mathcal{F}$ $\mathcal{F}$ $\mathcal{F}$ $\mathcal{F}$ $\mathcal{F}$ $\mathcal{F}$

f f f f f f f f f f f f f

f f f f f f f f f f f f f

f f f f f f f f f f f f f

f f f f f f f f f f f f f

f f f f f f f f f f f f f

Trace the letter Ff.

$\mathscr{F}$ f Flexible

$\mathscr{F}$ $\mathscr{F}$ $\mathscr{F}$ $\mathscr{F}$ $\mathscr{F}$ $\mathscr{F}$ $\mathscr{F}$ $\mathscr{F}$ $\mathscr{F}$ $\mathscr{F}$ $\mathscr{F}$ $\mathscr{F}$ $\mathscr{F}$ $\mathscr{F}$

$\mathscr{F}$ $\mathscr{F}$ $\mathscr{F}$ $\mathscr{F}$ $\mathscr{F}$ $\mathscr{F}$ $\mathscr{F}$ $\mathscr{F}$ $\mathscr{F}$ $\mathscr{F}$ $\mathscr{F}$ $\mathscr{F}$ $\mathscr{F}$

$\mathscr{F}$ $\mathscr{F}$ $\mathscr{F}$ $\mathscr{F}$ $\mathscr{F}$ $\mathscr{F}$ $\mathscr{F}$ $\mathscr{F}$ $\mathscr{F}$ $\mathscr{F}$ $\mathscr{F}$ $\mathscr{F}$ $\mathscr{F}$

$\mathscr{F}$ $\mathscr{F}$ $\mathscr{F}$ $\mathscr{F}$ $\mathscr{F}$ $\mathscr{F}$ $\mathscr{F}$ $\mathscr{F}$ $\mathscr{F}$ $\mathscr{F}$ $\mathscr{F}$ $\mathscr{F}$ $\mathscr{F}$

$\mathscr{F}$ $\mathscr{F}$ $\mathscr{F}$ $\mathscr{F}$ $\mathscr{F}$ $\mathscr{F}$ $\mathscr{F}$ $\mathscr{F}$ $\mathscr{F}$ $\mathscr{F}$ $\mathscr{F}$ $\mathscr{F}$ $\mathscr{F}$

$\mathscr{F}$ $\mathscr{F}$ $\mathscr{F}$ $\mathscr{F}$ $\mathscr{F}$ $\mathscr{F}$ $\mathscr{F}$ $\mathscr{F}$ $\mathscr{F}$ $\mathscr{F}$ $\mathscr{F}$ $\mathscr{F}$ $\mathscr{F}$

f f f f f f f f f f f f f

f f f f f f f f f f f f f

f f f f f f f f f f f f f

f f f f f f f f f f f f f

f f f f f f f f f f f f f

Trace the letter Ff. Then write the letter Ff as many times as possible.

$\mathcal{F}f$ $\mathcal{F}avorite$

$\mathcal{F}$ $\mathcal{F}$ $\mathcal{F}$

$\mathcal{F}$ $\mathcal{F}$ $\mathcal{F}$

$\mathcal{F}$ $\mathcal{F}$ $\mathcal{F}$

$\mathcal{F}$ $\mathcal{F}$ $\mathcal{F}$

$\mathcal{F}$ $\mathcal{F}$ $\mathcal{F}$

$\mathcal{F}$ $\mathcal{F}$ $\mathcal{F}$

f f f

f f f

f f f

f f f

f f f

Learn to Write in Cursive: Handwriting Practice Workbook

Write the sentence onto the lines below. Then trace and write the letters.

F was a fan

Made of beautiful stuff,

And when it was used,

It went puffy puff puff!

F F F

F F F

f f f

f f f

Trace the letter Gg.

G g   Gaggle

Learn to Write in Cursive: Handwriting Practice Workbook

Trace the letter Gg.

$\mathcal{G}$ g   Generosity

$\mathcal{G}$ $\mathcal{G}$ $\mathcal{G}$ $\mathcal{G}$ $\mathcal{G}$ $\mathcal{G}$ $\mathcal{G}$ $\mathcal{G}$ $\mathcal{G}$ $\mathcal{G}$ $\mathcal{G}$

$\mathcal{G}$ $\mathcal{G}$ $\mathcal{G}$ $\mathcal{G}$ $\mathcal{G}$ $\mathcal{G}$ $\mathcal{G}$ $\mathcal{G}$ $\mathcal{G}$ $\mathcal{G}$ $\mathcal{G}$

$\mathcal{G}$ $\mathcal{G}$ $\mathcal{G}$ $\mathcal{G}$ $\mathcal{G}$ $\mathcal{G}$ $\mathcal{G}$ $\mathcal{G}$ $\mathcal{G}$ $\mathcal{G}$ $\mathcal{G}$

$\mathcal{G}$ $\mathcal{G}$ $\mathcal{G}$ $\mathcal{G}$ $\mathcal{G}$ $\mathcal{G}$ $\mathcal{G}$ $\mathcal{G}$ $\mathcal{G}$ $\mathcal{G}$ $\mathcal{G}$

$\mathcal{G}$ $\mathcal{G}$ $\mathcal{G}$ $\mathcal{G}$ $\mathcal{G}$ $\mathcal{G}$ $\mathcal{G}$ $\mathcal{G}$ $\mathcal{G}$ $\mathcal{G}$ $\mathcal{G}$

$\mathcal{G}$ $\mathcal{G}$ $\mathcal{G}$ $\mathcal{G}$ $\mathcal{G}$ $\mathcal{G}$ $\mathcal{G}$ $\mathcal{G}$ $\mathcal{G}$ $\mathcal{G}$ $\mathcal{G}$

g g g g g g g g g g g

g g g g g g g g g g g

g g g g g g g g g g g

g g g g g g g g g g g

g g g g g g g g g g g

Trace the letter Gg. Then write the letter Gg as many times as possible.

G g   Gather

Learn to Write in Cursive: Handwriting Practice Workbook

Write the sentence onto the lines below. Then trace and write the letters.

G was a gooseberry,

Perfectly red;

To be made into jam,

And eaten with bread.

G G G G

G G G G

g g g

g g g

Trace the letter Hh.

$\mathcal{H}$ h　$\mathcal{H}eehaw$

$\mathcal{H}$ $\mathcal{H}$ $\mathcal{H}$ $\mathcal{H}$ $\mathcal{H}$ $\mathcal{H}$ $\mathcal{H}$ $\mathcal{H}$ $\mathcal{H}$ $\mathcal{H}$ $\mathcal{H}$ $\mathcal{H}$ $\mathcal{H}$

$\mathcal{H}$ $\mathcal{H}$ $\mathcal{H}$ $\mathcal{H}$ $\mathcal{H}$ $\mathcal{H}$ $\mathcal{H}$ $\mathcal{H}$ $\mathcal{H}$ $\mathcal{H}$ $\mathcal{H}$ $\mathcal{H}$ $\mathcal{H}$

$\mathcal{H}$ $\mathcal{H}$ $\mathcal{H}$ $\mathcal{H}$ $\mathcal{H}$ $\mathcal{H}$ $\mathcal{H}$ $\mathcal{H}$ $\mathcal{H}$ $\mathcal{H}$ $\mathcal{H}$ $\mathcal{H}$ $\mathcal{H}$

$\mathcal{H}$ $\mathcal{H}$ $\mathcal{H}$ $\mathcal{H}$ $\mathcal{H}$ $\mathcal{H}$ $\mathcal{H}$ $\mathcal{H}$ $\mathcal{H}$ $\mathcal{H}$ $\mathcal{H}$ $\mathcal{H}$ $\mathcal{H}$

$\mathcal{H}$ $\mathcal{H}$ $\mathcal{H}$ $\mathcal{H}$ $\mathcal{H}$ $\mathcal{H}$ $\mathcal{H}$ $\mathcal{H}$ $\mathcal{H}$ $\mathcal{H}$ $\mathcal{H}$ $\mathcal{H}$ $\mathcal{H}$

$\mathcal{H}$ $\mathcal{H}$ $\mathcal{H}$ $\mathcal{H}$ $\mathcal{H}$ $\mathcal{H}$ $\mathcal{H}$ $\mathcal{H}$ $\mathcal{H}$ $\mathcal{H}$ $\mathcal{H}$ $\mathcal{H}$ $\mathcal{H}$

h h h h h h h h h h

h h h h h h h h h h

h h h h h h h h h h

h h h h h h h h h h

h h h h h h h h h h

Trace the letter Hh.

$\mathcal{H}$ h $\mathcal{H}ardship$

$\mathcal{H}$ $\mathcal{H}$ $\mathcal{H}$ $\mathcal{H}$ $\mathcal{H}$ $\mathcal{H}$ $\mathcal{H}$ $\mathcal{H}$ $\mathcal{H}$ $\mathcal{H}$ $\mathcal{H}$ $\mathcal{H}$ $\mathcal{H}$ $\mathcal{H}$

$\mathcal{H}$ $\mathcal{H}$ $\mathcal{H}$ $\mathcal{H}$ $\mathcal{H}$ $\mathcal{H}$ $\mathcal{H}$ $\mathcal{H}$ $\mathcal{H}$ $\mathcal{H}$ $\mathcal{H}$ $\mathcal{H}$ $\mathcal{H}$

$\mathcal{H}$ $\mathcal{H}$ $\mathcal{H}$ $\mathcal{H}$ $\mathcal{H}$ $\mathcal{H}$ $\mathcal{H}$ $\mathcal{H}$ $\mathcal{H}$ $\mathcal{H}$ $\mathcal{H}$ $\mathcal{H}$ $\mathcal{H}$

$\mathcal{H}$ $\mathcal{H}$ $\mathcal{H}$ $\mathcal{H}$ $\mathcal{H}$ $\mathcal{H}$ $\mathcal{H}$ $\mathcal{H}$ $\mathcal{H}$ $\mathcal{H}$ $\mathcal{H}$ $\mathcal{H}$ $\mathcal{H}$

$\mathcal{H}$ $\mathcal{H}$ $\mathcal{H}$ $\mathcal{H}$ $\mathcal{H}$ $\mathcal{H}$ $\mathcal{H}$ $\mathcal{H}$ $\mathcal{H}$ $\mathcal{H}$ $\mathcal{H}$ $\mathcal{H}$

$\mathcal{H}$ $\mathcal{H}$ $\mathcal{H}$ $\mathcal{H}$ $\mathcal{H}$ $\mathcal{H}$ $\mathcal{H}$ $\mathcal{H}$ $\mathcal{H}$ $\mathcal{H}$ $\mathcal{H}$ $\mathcal{H}$

h h h h h h h h h h

h h h h h h h h h h

h h h h h h h h h h

h h h h h h h h h h

h h h h h h h h h h

Trace the letter Hh. Then write the letter Hh as many times as possible.

H h Health

H H H

H H H

H H H

H H H

H H H

H H H

h h h

h h h

h h h

h h h

h h h

Learn to Write in Cursive: Handwriting Practice Workbook

Write the sentence onto the lines below. Then trace and write the letters.

H was a heron,

Who stood in a stream:

The length of his neck

And his legs was extreme.

H H H H

H H H H

h h h h

h h h h

Trace the letter Ii.

Ii Insight

Trace the letter Ii.

Ii Instant

Trace the letter Ii. Then write the letter Ii as many times as possible.

Ii Itchy

Write the sentence onto the lines below. Then trace and write the letters.

I was an inkstand,

Which stood on a table,

With a pen to write with

When we are able.

el el el

el el el

i i i

i i i

Trace the letter Jj.

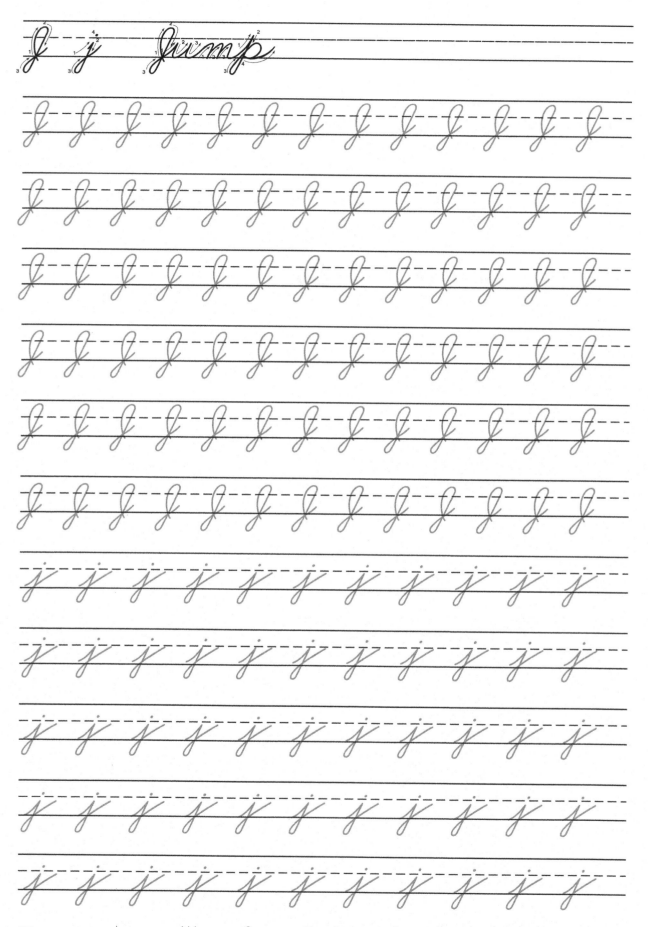

Learn to Write in Cursive: Handwriting Practice Workbook

Trace the letter Jj.

Trace the letter Jj. Then write the letter Jj as many times as possible.

J J j Juggle

J J J

J J J

J J J

J J J

J J J

J J J

j j j

j j j

j j j

j j j

j j j

Write the sentence onto the lines below. Then trace and write the letters.

I was a jug,

So pretty and white,

With fresh water in it

At morning and night.

J J J

J J J

j j j

j j j

Trace the letter Kk.

Kk Kangaroo

𝒦 𝒦 𝒦 𝒦 𝒦 𝒦 𝒦 𝒦 𝒦 𝒦 𝒦

𝒦 𝒦 𝒦 𝒦 𝒦 𝒦 𝒦 𝒦 𝒦 𝒦 𝒦

𝒦 𝒦 𝒦 𝒦 𝒦 𝒦 𝒦 𝒦 𝒦 𝒦 𝒦

𝒦 𝒦 𝒦 𝒦 𝒦 𝒦 𝒦 𝒦 𝒦 𝒦 𝒦

𝒦 𝒦 𝒦 𝒦 𝒦 𝒦 𝒦 𝒦 𝒦 𝒦 𝒦

𝒦 𝒦 𝒦 𝒦 𝒦 𝒦 𝒦 𝒦 𝒦 𝒦 𝒦

𝓀 𝓀 𝓀 𝓀 𝓀 𝓀 𝓀 𝓀 𝓀 𝓀

𝓀 𝓀 𝓀 𝓀 𝓀 𝓀 𝓀 𝓀 𝓀 𝓀 𝓀

𝓀 𝓀 𝓀 𝓀 𝓀 𝓀 𝓀 𝓀 𝓀 𝓀 𝓀

𝓀 𝓀 𝓀 𝓀 𝓀 𝓀 𝓀 𝓀 𝓀 𝓀 𝓀

𝓀 𝓀 𝓀 𝓀 𝓀 𝓀 𝓀 𝓀 𝓀 𝓀 𝓀

Trace the letter Kk.

Kk $Kinfolk$

K K K K K K K K K K K K

K K K K K K K K K K K

K K K K K K K K K K K

K K K K K K K K K K K

K K K K K K K K K K K

K K K K K K K K K K K

k k k k k k k k k k

k k k k k k k k k k

k k k k k k k k k k

k k k k k k k k k k

k k k k k k k k k k k

Trace the letter Kk. Then write the letter Kk as many times as possible.

K k   Karate

K K K

K K K

K K K

K K K

K K K

K K K

k k k

k k k

k k k

k k k

k k k

Write the sentence onto the lines below. Then trace and write the letters.

K was a kingfisher:

Quickly he flew,

So bright and so pretty!

Green, purple, and blue.

K K K

K K K

k k k

k k k

Trace the letter Ll.

L l Lollipop

L L L L L L L L L L L L L

L L L L L L L L L L L L L

L L L L L L L L L L L L L

L L L L L L L L L L L L L

L L L L L L L L L L L L L

L L L L L L L L L L L L L

l l l l l l l l l l l l

l l l l l l l l l l l l l

l l l l l l l l l l l l l

l l l l l l l l l l l l l

l l l l l l l l l l l l l

Trace the letter Ll.

L l Learning

L L L L L L L L L L L L L

L L L L L L L L L L L L L

L L L L L L L L L L L L L

L L L L L L L L L L L L L

L L L L L L L L L L L L L

L L L L L L L L L L L L L

l l l l l l l l l l l l l

l l l l l l l l l l l l l

l l l l l l l l l l l l l

l l l l l l l l l l l l l

l l l l l l l l l l l l l

Trace the letter Ll. Then write the letter Ll as many times as possible.

$\mathcal{L}$ ℓ $\mathcal{L}egend$

$\mathcal{L}$ $\mathcal{L}$ $\mathcal{L}$ $\mathcal{L}$

$\mathcal{L}$ $\mathcal{L}$ $\mathcal{L}$

$\mathcal{L}$ $\mathcal{L}$ $\mathcal{L}$

$\mathcal{L}$ $\mathcal{L}$ $\mathcal{L}$

$\mathcal{L}$ $\mathcal{L}$ $\mathcal{L}$

$\mathcal{L}$ $\mathcal{L}$ $\mathcal{L}$

ℓ ℓ ℓ

ℓ ℓ ℓ

ℓ ℓ ℓ

ℓ ℓ ℓ

ℓ ℓ ℓ

Learn to Write in Cursive: Handwriting Practice Workbook

Write the sentence onto the lines below. Then trace and write the letters.

L was a lily,

So white and so sweet!

To see it and smell it

Was quite a nice treat.

L L L

L L L

l l l

l l l

Trace the letter Mm.

$\mathcal{M}$ m $\mathcal{M}ammal$

$\mathcal{M}$ $\mathcal{M}$ $\mathcal{M}$ $\mathcal{M}$ $\mathcal{M}$ $\mathcal{M}$ $\mathcal{M}$ $\mathcal{M}$ $\mathcal{M}$ $\mathcal{M}$

$\mathcal{M}$ $\mathcal{M}$ $\mathcal{M}$ $\mathcal{M}$ $\mathcal{M}$ $\mathcal{M}$ $\mathcal{M}$ $\mathcal{M}$ $\mathcal{M}$ $\mathcal{M}$

$\mathcal{M}$ $\mathcal{M}$ $\mathcal{M}$ $\mathcal{M}$ $\mathcal{M}$ $\mathcal{M}$ $\mathcal{M}$ $\mathcal{M}$ $\mathcal{M}$ $\mathcal{M}$

$\mathcal{M}$ $\mathcal{M}$ $\mathcal{M}$ $\mathcal{M}$ $\mathcal{M}$ $\mathcal{M}$ $\mathcal{M}$ $\mathcal{M}$ $\mathcal{M}$ $\mathcal{M}$

$\mathcal{M}$ $\mathcal{M}$ $\mathcal{M}$ $\mathcal{M}$ $\mathcal{M}$ $\mathcal{M}$ $\mathcal{M}$ $\mathcal{M}$ $\mathcal{M}$ $\mathcal{M}$

$\mathcal{M}$ $\mathcal{M}$ $\mathcal{M}$ $\mathcal{M}$ $\mathcal{M}$ $\mathcal{M}$ $\mathcal{M}$ $\mathcal{M}$ $\mathcal{M}$ $\mathcal{M}$

m m m m m m m m m m

m m m m m m m m m m

m m m m m m m m m m

m m m m m m m m m m

m m m m m m m m m m

Learn to Write in Cursive: Handwriting Practice Workbook

Trace the letter Mm.

M m m Mountain

m m m m m m m m m m

m m m m m m m m m m

m m m m m m m m m m

m m m m m m m m m m

m m m m m m m m m m

m m m m m m m m m m

m m m m m m m m m

m m m m m m m m m

m m m m m m m m m m

m m m m m m m m m m

m m m m m m m m m m

Trace the letter Mm. Then write the letter Mm as many times as possible.

$\mathcal{M}$ m $\mathcal{M}amatee$

$\mathcal{M}$ $\mathcal{M}$ $\mathcal{M}$

$\mathcal{M}$ $\mathcal{M}$ $\mathcal{M}$

$\mathcal{M}$ $\mathcal{M}$ $\mathcal{M}$

$\mathcal{M}$ $\mathcal{M}$ $\mathcal{M}$

$\mathcal{M}$ $\mathcal{M}$ $\mathcal{M}$

$\mathcal{M}$ $\mathcal{M}$ $\mathcal{M}$

m m m

m m m

m m m

m m m

m m m

Write the sentence onto the lines below. Then trace and write the letters.

M was a man,

Who walked all around;

And he wore a long coat

That reached the ground.

m m m

m m m

m m m

m m m

Trace the letter Nn.

$\mathcal{N}$ n n Nocturnal

Learn to Write in Cursive: Handwriting Practice Workbook

Trace the letter Nn.

$\mathcal{N}$ n $\mathcal{N}ation$

n n n n n n n n n n n n n n

n n n n n n n n n n n n n n

n n n n n n n n n n n n n n

n n n n n n n n n n n n n n

n n n n n n n n n n n n n n

n n n n n n n n n n n n n n

$\mathcal{N}$ $\mathcal{N}$ $\mathcal{N}$ $\mathcal{N}$ $\mathcal{N}$ $\mathcal{N}$ $\mathcal{N}$ $\mathcal{N}$ $\mathcal{N}$ $\mathcal{N}$ $\mathcal{N}$ $\mathcal{N}$

$\mathcal{N}$ $\mathcal{N}$ $\mathcal{N}$ $\mathcal{N}$ $\mathcal{N}$ $\mathcal{N}$ $\mathcal{N}$ $\mathcal{N}$ $\mathcal{N}$ $\mathcal{N}$ $\mathcal{N}$ $\mathcal{N}$

$\mathcal{N}$ $\mathcal{N}$ $\mathcal{N}$ $\mathcal{N}$ $\mathcal{N}$ $\mathcal{N}$ $\mathcal{N}$ $\mathcal{N}$ $\mathcal{N}$ $\mathcal{N}$ $\mathcal{N}$ $\mathcal{N}$

$\mathcal{N}$ $\mathcal{N}$ $\mathcal{N}$ $\mathcal{N}$ $\mathcal{N}$ $\mathcal{N}$ $\mathcal{N}$ $\mathcal{N}$ $\mathcal{N}$ $\mathcal{N}$ $\mathcal{N}$ $\mathcal{N}$

$\mathcal{N}$ $\mathcal{N}$ $\mathcal{N}$ $\mathcal{N}$ $\mathcal{N}$ $\mathcal{N}$ $\mathcal{N}$ $\mathcal{N}$ $\mathcal{N}$ $\mathcal{N}$ $\mathcal{N}$ $\mathcal{N}$

Trace the letter Nn. Then write the letter Nn as many times as possible.

$\mathcal{N}$ $\mathcal{N}$ n $\mathcal{N}anny$

n n n

n n n

n n n

n n n

n n n

n n n

n n n

n n n

n n n

n n n

n n n

Learn to Write in Cursive: Handwriting Practice Workbook

Write the sentence onto the lines below. Then trace and write the letters.

N was a nut

So smooth and so brown!

And when it was ripe,

It fell tumble-dum-down.

n n n

n n n

n n n

n n n

Trace the letter Oo.

Learn to Write in Cursive: Handwriting Practice Workbook

Trace the letter Oo.

Trace the letter Oo. Then write the letter Oo as many times as possible.

$\mathcal{O}$ o $\mathcal{Oxygen}$

$\mathcal{O}$ $\mathcal{O}$ $\mathcal{O}$

$\mathcal{O}$ $\mathcal{O}$ $\mathcal{O}$

$\mathcal{O}$ $\mathcal{O}$ $\mathcal{O}$

$\mathcal{O}$ $\mathcal{O}$ $\mathcal{O}$

$\mathcal{O}$ $\mathcal{O}$ $\mathcal{O}$

$\mathcal{O}$ $\mathcal{O}$ $\mathcal{O}$

o o o

o o o

o o o

o o o

o o o

Write the sentence onto the lines below. Then trace and write the letters.

O was an oyster,

Who lived in his shell:

If you let him alone,

He felt perfectly well.

O O O

O O O

o o o

o o o

Trace the letter Pp.

Learn to Write in Cursive: Handwriting Practice Workbook

Trace the letter Pp.

Trace the letter Pp. Then write the letter Pp as many times as possible.

$P p \quad Papyrus$

Learn to Write in Cursive: Handwriting Practice Workbook

Write the sentence onto the lines below. Then trace and write the letters.

P was a polly,

All red, blue, and green,

The most beautiful polly

That ever was seen.

P P P

P P P

p p p

p p p

Trace the letter Qq.

Learn to Write in Cursive: Handwriting Practice Workbook

Trace the letter Qq.

Trace the letter Qq. Then write the letter Qq as many times as possible.

Q q Quaking

Q Q Q

Q Q Q

Q Q Q

Q Q Q

Q Q Q

Q Q Q

q q q

q q q

q q q

q q q

q q q

Learn to Write in Cursive: Handwriting Practice Workbook

Write the sentence onto the lines below. Then trace and write the letters.

Q was a quill

Made into a pen;

But I do not know where,

And I cannot say when.

Q Q Q

Q Q Q

q q q

q q q

Trace the letter Rr.

R r Racquet

Learn to Write in Cursive: Handwriting Practice Workbook

Trace the letter Rr.

$\mathcal{R}$ $\mathcal{r}$ $\mathcal{Regular}$

$\mathcal{R}$ $\mathcal{R}$ $\mathcal{R}$ $\mathcal{R}$ $\mathcal{R}$ $\mathcal{R}$ $\mathcal{R}$ $\mathcal{R}$ $\mathcal{R}$ $\mathcal{R}$

$\mathcal{R}$ $\mathcal{R}$ $\mathcal{R}$ $\mathcal{R}$ $\mathcal{R}$ $\mathcal{R}$ $\mathcal{R}$ $\mathcal{R}$ $\mathcal{R}$ $\mathcal{R}$

$\mathcal{R}$ $\mathcal{R}$ $\mathcal{R}$ $\mathcal{R}$ $\mathcal{R}$ $\mathcal{R}$ $\mathcal{R}$ $\mathcal{R}$ $\mathcal{R}$ $\mathcal{R}$

$\mathcal{R}$ $\mathcal{R}$ $\mathcal{R}$ $\mathcal{R}$ $\mathcal{R}$ $\mathcal{R}$ $\mathcal{R}$ $\mathcal{R}$ $\mathcal{R}$ $\mathcal{R}$

$\mathcal{R}$ $\mathcal{R}$ $\mathcal{R}$ $\mathcal{R}$ $\mathcal{R}$ $\mathcal{R}$ $\mathcal{R}$ $\mathcal{R}$ $\mathcal{R}$ $\mathcal{R}$

$\mathcal{R}$ $\mathcal{R}$ $\mathcal{R}$ $\mathcal{R}$ $\mathcal{R}$ $\mathcal{R}$ $\mathcal{R}$ $\mathcal{R}$ $\mathcal{R}$ $\mathcal{R}$

$\mathcal{r}$ $\mathcal{r}$ $\mathcal{r}$ $\mathcal{r}$ $\mathcal{r}$ $\mathcal{r}$ $\mathcal{r}$ $\mathcal{r}$ $\mathcal{r}$ $\mathcal{r}$

$\mathcal{r}$ $\mathcal{r}$ $\mathcal{r}$ $\mathcal{r}$ $\mathcal{r}$ $\mathcal{r}$ $\mathcal{r}$ $\mathcal{r}$ $\mathcal{r}$ $\mathcal{r}$

$\mathcal{r}$ $\mathcal{r}$ $\mathcal{r}$ $\mathcal{r}$ $\mathcal{r}$ $\mathcal{r}$ $\mathcal{r}$ $\mathcal{r}$ $\mathcal{r}$ $\mathcal{r}$

$\mathcal{r}$ $\mathcal{r}$ $\mathcal{r}$ $\mathcal{r}$ $\mathcal{r}$ $\mathcal{r}$ $\mathcal{r}$ $\mathcal{r}$ $\mathcal{r}$ $\mathcal{r}$

$\mathcal{r}$ $\mathcal{r}$ $\mathcal{r}$ $\mathcal{r}$ $\mathcal{r}$ $\mathcal{r}$ $\mathcal{r}$ $\mathcal{r}$ $\mathcal{r}$ $\mathcal{r}$

Trace the letter Rr. Then write the letter Rr as many times as possible.

R r   Ragweed

Learn to Write in Cursive: Handwriting Practice Workbook

Write the sentence onto the lines below. Then trace and write the letters.

R was a rattlesnake,

Rolled up so tight,

Those who saw him ran

For fear he should bite.

R R R

R R R

N N N

N N N

Trace the letter Ss.

$\mathcal{S}$ s $\mathcal{Sunshine}$

Learn to Write in Cursive: Handwriting Practice Workbook

Trace the letter Ss.

$\mathcal{S}$ s Saltfish

$\mathcal{S}$ $\mathcal{S}$ $\mathcal{S}$ $\mathcal{S}$ $\mathcal{S}$ $\mathcal{S}$ $\mathcal{S}$ $\mathcal{S}$ $\mathcal{S}$ $\mathcal{S}$

$\mathcal{S}$ $\mathcal{S}$ $\mathcal{S}$ $\mathcal{S}$ $\mathcal{S}$ $\mathcal{S}$ $\mathcal{S}$ $\mathcal{S}$ $\mathcal{S}$ $\mathcal{S}$

$\mathcal{S}$ $\mathcal{S}$ $\mathcal{S}$ $\mathcal{S}$ $\mathcal{S}$ $\mathcal{S}$ $\mathcal{S}$ $\mathcal{S}$ $\mathcal{S}$ $\mathcal{S}$

$\mathcal{S}$ $\mathcal{S}$ $\mathcal{S}$ $\mathcal{S}$ $\mathcal{S}$ $\mathcal{S}$ $\mathcal{S}$ $\mathcal{S}$ $\mathcal{S}$ $\mathcal{S}$

$\mathcal{S}$ $\mathcal{S}$ $\mathcal{S}$ $\mathcal{S}$ $\mathcal{S}$ $\mathcal{S}$ $\mathcal{S}$ $\mathcal{S}$ $\mathcal{S}$ $\mathcal{S}$

$\mathcal{S}$ $\mathcal{S}$ $\mathcal{S}$ $\mathcal{S}$ $\mathcal{S}$ $\mathcal{S}$ $\mathcal{S}$ $\mathcal{S}$ $\mathcal{S}$ $\mathcal{S}$

s s s s s s s s s s s

s s s s s s s s s s s

s s s s s s s s s s s

s s s s s s s s s s s

s s s s s s s s s s s

Trace the letter Ss. Then write the letter Ss as many times as possible.

$\mathcal{S}\ \mathcal{s}$ Saucers

Learn to Write in Cursive: Handwriting Practice Workbook

Write the sentence onto the lines below. Then trace and write the letters.

S was a screw

To screw down a box;

And then it was fastened

Without any locks.

S S S

S S S

S S S

S S S

Trace the letter Tt.

T t Teapot

F F F F F F F F F F F F F F
F F F F F F F F F F F F F F
F F F F F F F F F F F F F F
F F F F F F F F F F F F F F
F F F F F F F F F F F F F F
F F F F F F F F F F F F F F

t t t t t t t t t t t t t
t t t t t t t t t t t t t t
t t t t t t t t t t t t t t
t t t t t t t t t t t t t t
t t t t t t t t t t t t t t

Trace the letter Tt.

T t   Transport

$\mathcal{T}$ $\mathcal{T}$ $\mathcal{T}$ $\mathcal{T}$ $\mathcal{T}$ $\mathcal{T}$ $\mathcal{T}$ $\mathcal{T}$ $\mathcal{T}$ $\mathcal{T}$ $\mathcal{T}$ $\mathcal{T}$

$\mathcal{T}$ $\mathcal{T}$ $\mathcal{T}$ $\mathcal{T}$ $\mathcal{T}$ $\mathcal{T}$ $\mathcal{T}$ $\mathcal{T}$ $\mathcal{T}$ $\mathcal{T}$ $\mathcal{T}$ $\mathcal{T}$

$\mathcal{T}$ $\mathcal{T}$ $\mathcal{T}$ $\mathcal{T}$ $\mathcal{T}$ $\mathcal{T}$ $\mathcal{T}$ $\mathcal{T}$ $\mathcal{T}$ $\mathcal{T}$ $\mathcal{T}$ $\mathcal{T}$

$\mathcal{T}$ $\mathcal{T}$ $\mathcal{T}$ $\mathcal{T}$ $\mathcal{T}$ $\mathcal{T}$ $\mathcal{T}$ $\mathcal{T}$ $\mathcal{T}$ $\mathcal{T}$ $\mathcal{T}$ $\mathcal{T}$

$\mathcal{T}$ $\mathcal{T}$ $\mathcal{T}$ $\mathcal{T}$ $\mathcal{T}$ $\mathcal{T}$ $\mathcal{T}$ $\mathcal{T}$ $\mathcal{T}$ $\mathcal{T}$ $\mathcal{T}$ $\mathcal{T}$

$\mathcal{T}$ $\mathcal{T}$ $\mathcal{T}$ $\mathcal{T}$ $\mathcal{T}$ $\mathcal{T}$ $\mathcal{T}$ $\mathcal{T}$ $\mathcal{T}$ $\mathcal{T}$ $\mathcal{T}$ $\mathcal{T}$

t t t t t t t t t t t t t

t t t t t t t t t t t t t

t t t t t t t t t t t t t

t t t t t t t t t t t t t

t t t t t t t t t t t t t

Trace the letter Tt. Then write the letter Tt as many times as possible.

$\mathcal{T}t$ $\mathcal{T}axicab$

$\mathcal{T}$ $\mathcal{T}$ $\mathcal{T}$

$\mathcal{T}$ $\mathcal{T}$ $\mathcal{T}$

$\mathcal{T}$ $\mathcal{T}$ $\mathcal{T}$

$\mathcal{T}$ $\mathcal{T}$ $\mathcal{T}$

$\mathcal{T}$ $\mathcal{T}$ $\mathcal{T}$

$\mathcal{T}$ $\mathcal{T}$ $\mathcal{T}$

t t t

t t t

t t t

t t t

t t t

Learn to Write in Cursive: Handwriting Practice Workbook

Write the sentence onto the lines below. Then trace and write the letters.

T was a thimble,

Of silver so bright!

When placed on the finger,

It fitted so tight!

F F F

F F F

t t t

t t t

Trace the letter Uu.

U u Unstruck

Learn to Write in Cursive: Handwriting Practice Workbook

Trace the letter Uu.

Uu Under

$\mathcal{U}$ $\mathcal{U}$ $\mathcal{U}$ $\mathcal{U}$ $\mathcal{U}$ $\mathcal{U}$ $\mathcal{U}$ $\mathcal{U}$ $\mathcal{U}$ $\mathcal{U}$

$\mathcal{U}$ $\mathcal{U}$ $\mathcal{U}$ $\mathcal{U}$ $\mathcal{U}$ $\mathcal{U}$ $\mathcal{U}$ $\mathcal{U}$ $\mathcal{U}$ $\mathcal{U}$

$\mathcal{U}$ $\mathcal{U}$ $\mathcal{U}$ $\mathcal{U}$ $\mathcal{U}$ $\mathcal{U}$ $\mathcal{U}$ $\mathcal{U}$ $\mathcal{U}$ $\mathcal{U}$

$\mathcal{U}$ $\mathcal{U}$ $\mathcal{U}$ $\mathcal{U}$ $\mathcal{U}$ $\mathcal{U}$ $\mathcal{U}$ $\mathcal{U}$ $\mathcal{U}$ $\mathcal{U}$

$\mathcal{U}$ $\mathcal{U}$ $\mathcal{U}$ $\mathcal{U}$ $\mathcal{U}$ $\mathcal{U}$ $\mathcal{U}$ $\mathcal{U}$ $\mathcal{U}$ $\mathcal{U}$

$\mathcal{U}$ $\mathcal{U}$ $\mathcal{U}$ $\mathcal{U}$ $\mathcal{U}$ $\mathcal{U}$ $\mathcal{U}$ $\mathcal{U}$ $\mathcal{U}$ $\mathcal{U}$

u u u u u u u u u u

u u u u u u u u u u

u u u u u u u u u u

u u u u u u u u u u

u u u u u u u u u u

Trace the letter Uu. Then write the letter Uu as many times as possible.

U u Unwound

U U U

U U U

U U U

U U U

U U U

U U U

u u u

u u u

u u u

u u u

u u u

Learn to Write in Cursive: Handwriting Practice Workbook

Write the sentence onto the lines below. Then trace and write the letters.

It was an upper-coat,

Woolly and warm,

To wear over all

In the snow or the storm.

U   U   U

U   U   U

u   u   u

u   u   u

Trace the letter Vv.

$\mathcal{V}$ $\mathcal{v}$ $\mathcal{Valve}$

$\mathcal{V}$ $\mathcal{V}$ $\mathcal{V}$ $\mathcal{V}$ $\mathcal{V}$ $\mathcal{V}$ $\mathcal{V}$ $\mathcal{V}$ $\mathcal{V}$ $\mathcal{V}$ $\mathcal{V}$ $\mathcal{V}$ $\mathcal{V}$ $\mathcal{V}$

$\mathcal{V}$ $\mathcal{V}$ $\mathcal{V}$ $\mathcal{V}$ $\mathcal{V}$ $\mathcal{V}$ $\mathcal{V}$ $\mathcal{V}$ $\mathcal{V}$ $\mathcal{V}$ $\mathcal{V}$ $\mathcal{V}$ $\mathcal{V}$ $\mathcal{V}$

$\mathcal{V}$ $\mathcal{V}$ $\mathcal{V}$ $\mathcal{V}$ $\mathcal{V}$ $\mathcal{V}$ $\mathcal{V}$ $\mathcal{V}$ $\mathcal{V}$ $\mathcal{V}$ $\mathcal{V}$ $\mathcal{V}$ $\mathcal{V}$ $\mathcal{V}$

$\mathcal{V}$ $\mathcal{V}$ $\mathcal{V}$ $\mathcal{V}$ $\mathcal{V}$ $\mathcal{V}$ $\mathcal{V}$ $\mathcal{V}$ $\mathcal{V}$ $\mathcal{V}$ $\mathcal{V}$ $\mathcal{V}$ $\mathcal{V}$ $\mathcal{V}$

$\mathcal{V}$ $\mathcal{V}$ $\mathcal{V}$ $\mathcal{V}$ $\mathcal{V}$ $\mathcal{V}$ $\mathcal{V}$ $\mathcal{V}$ $\mathcal{V}$ $\mathcal{V}$ $\mathcal{V}$ $\mathcal{V}$ $\mathcal{V}$ $\mathcal{V}$

$\mathcal{V}$ $\mathcal{V}$ $\mathcal{V}$ $\mathcal{V}$ $\mathcal{V}$ $\mathcal{V}$ $\mathcal{V}$ $\mathcal{V}$ $\mathcal{V}$ $\mathcal{V}$ $\mathcal{V}$ $\mathcal{V}$ $\mathcal{V}$ $\mathcal{V}$

v v v v v v v v v v v v

v v v v v v v v v v v

v v v v v v v v v v v

v v v v v v v v v v v v

v v v v v v v v v v v

Trace the letter Vv.

$\mathcal{V}$ $\mathcal{v}$ $\mathcal{Verse}$

$\mathcal{V}$ $\mathcal{V}$ $\mathcal{V}$ $\mathcal{V}$ $\mathcal{V}$ $\mathcal{V}$ $\mathcal{V}$ $\mathcal{V}$ $\mathcal{V}$ $\mathcal{V}$ $\mathcal{V}$ $\mathcal{V}$ $\mathcal{V}$ $\mathcal{V}$

$\mathcal{V}$ $\mathcal{V}$ $\mathcal{V}$ $\mathcal{V}$ $\mathcal{V}$ $\mathcal{V}$ $\mathcal{V}$ $\mathcal{V}$ $\mathcal{V}$ $\mathcal{V}$ $\mathcal{V}$ $\mathcal{V}$ $\mathcal{V}$ $\mathcal{V}$

$\mathcal{V}$ $\mathcal{V}$ $\mathcal{V}$ $\mathcal{V}$ $\mathcal{V}$ $\mathcal{V}$ $\mathcal{V}$ $\mathcal{V}$ $\mathcal{V}$ $\mathcal{V}$ $\mathcal{V}$ $\mathcal{V}$ $\mathcal{V}$ $\mathcal{V}$

$\mathcal{V}$ $\mathcal{V}$ $\mathcal{V}$ $\mathcal{V}$ $\mathcal{V}$ $\mathcal{V}$ $\mathcal{V}$ $\mathcal{V}$ $\mathcal{V}$ $\mathcal{V}$ $\mathcal{V}$ $\mathcal{V}$ $\mathcal{V}$ $\mathcal{V}$

$\mathcal{V}$ $\mathcal{V}$ $\mathcal{V}$ $\mathcal{V}$ $\mathcal{V}$ $\mathcal{V}$ $\mathcal{V}$ $\mathcal{V}$ $\mathcal{V}$ $\mathcal{V}$ $\mathcal{V}$ $\mathcal{V}$ $\mathcal{V}$ $\mathcal{V}$

$\mathcal{V}$ $\mathcal{V}$ $\mathcal{V}$ $\mathcal{V}$ $\mathcal{V}$ $\mathcal{V}$ $\mathcal{V}$ $\mathcal{V}$ $\mathcal{V}$ $\mathcal{V}$ $\mathcal{V}$ $\mathcal{V}$ $\mathcal{V}$ $\mathcal{V}$

v v v v v v v v v v v v v

v v v v v v v v v v v v v

v v v v v v v v v v v v v

v v v v v v v v v v v v v

v v v v v v v v v v v v v

Trace the letter Vv. Then write the letter Vv as many times as possible.

$\mathcal{V}$ $\mathcal{v}$ Vacuum

$\mathcal{V}$ $\mathcal{V}$ $\mathcal{V}$

$\mathcal{V}$ $\mathcal{V}$ $\mathcal{V}$

$\mathcal{V}$ $\mathcal{V}$ $\mathcal{V}$

$\mathcal{V}$ $\mathcal{V}$ $\mathcal{V}$

$\mathcal{V}$ $\mathcal{V}$ $\mathcal{V}$

$\mathcal{V}$ $\mathcal{V}$ $\mathcal{V}$

$\mathcal{v}$ $\mathcal{v}$ $\mathcal{v}$

$\mathcal{v}$ $\mathcal{v}$ $\mathcal{v}$

$\mathcal{v}$ $\mathcal{v}$ $\mathcal{v}$

$\mathcal{v}$ $\mathcal{v}$ $\mathcal{v}$

$\mathcal{v}$ $\mathcal{v}$ $\mathcal{v}$

Write the sentence onto the lines below. Then trace and write the letters.

V was a veil

With a border upon it,

And a ribbon to tie it

All round a pink bonnet.

Trace the letter Ww.

W ur Wallour

Learn to Write in Cursive: Handwriting Practice Workbook

Trace the letter Ww.

W w Whistle

Write the sentence onto the lines below. Then trace and write the letters.

W w Weather

Learn to Write in Cursive: Handwriting Practice Workbook

Trace the letter Ww. Then write the letter Ww as many times as possible.

W was a watch,

Where, in letters of gold,

The hour of the day

You might always behold.

W W W

W W W

w w w

w w w

Trace the letter Xx.

$\mathcal{X}$ x $\mathcal{X}$erox

$\mathcal{X}$ $\mathcal{X}$ $\mathcal{X}$ $\mathcal{X}$ $\mathcal{X}$ $\mathcal{X}$ $\mathcal{X}$ $\mathcal{X}$ $\mathcal{X}$ $\mathcal{X}$ $\mathcal{X}$ $\mathcal{X}$ $\mathcal{X}$ $\mathcal{X}$

$\mathcal{X}$ $\mathcal{X}$ $\mathcal{X}$ $\mathcal{X}$ $\mathcal{X}$ $\mathcal{X}$ $\mathcal{X}$ $\mathcal{X}$ $\mathcal{X}$ $\mathcal{X}$ $\mathcal{X}$ $\mathcal{X}$ $\mathcal{X}$ $\mathcal{X}$

$\mathcal{X}$ $\mathcal{X}$ $\mathcal{X}$ $\mathcal{X}$ $\mathcal{X}$ $\mathcal{X}$ $\mathcal{X}$ $\mathcal{X}$ $\mathcal{X}$ $\mathcal{X}$ $\mathcal{X}$ $\mathcal{X}$ $\mathcal{X}$ $\mathcal{X}$

$\mathcal{X}$ $\mathcal{X}$ $\mathcal{X}$ $\mathcal{X}$ $\mathcal{X}$ $\mathcal{X}$ $\mathcal{X}$ $\mathcal{X}$ $\mathcal{X}$ $\mathcal{X}$ $\mathcal{X}$ $\mathcal{X}$ $\mathcal{X}$ $\mathcal{X}$

$\mathcal{X}$ $\mathcal{X}$ $\mathcal{X}$ $\mathcal{X}$ $\mathcal{X}$ $\mathcal{X}$ $\mathcal{X}$ $\mathcal{X}$ $\mathcal{X}$ $\mathcal{X}$ $\mathcal{X}$ $\mathcal{X}$ $\mathcal{X}$ $\mathcal{X}$

$\mathcal{X}$ $\mathcal{X}$ $\mathcal{X}$ $\mathcal{X}$ $\mathcal{X}$ $\mathcal{X}$ $\mathcal{X}$ $\mathcal{X}$ $\mathcal{X}$ $\mathcal{X}$ $\mathcal{X}$ $\mathcal{X}$ $\mathcal{X}$ $\mathcal{X}$

x x x x x x x x x x x x x

x x x x x x x x x x x x x

x x x x x x x x x x x x x

x x x x x x x x x x x x x

x x x x x x x x x x x x x

Trace the letter Xx.

X x Xylose

$\mathcal{X}$ $\mathcal{X}$ $\mathcal{X}$ $\mathcal{X}$ $\mathcal{X}$ $\mathcal{X}$ $\mathcal{X}$ $\mathcal{X}$ $\mathcal{X}$ $\mathcal{X}$ $\mathcal{X}$ $\mathcal{X}$ $\mathcal{X}$ $\mathcal{X}$ $\mathcal{X}$

$\mathcal{X}$ $\mathcal{X}$ $\mathcal{X}$ $\mathcal{X}$ $\mathcal{X}$ $\mathcal{X}$ $\mathcal{X}$ $\mathcal{X}$ $\mathcal{X}$ $\mathcal{X}$ $\mathcal{X}$ $\mathcal{X}$ $\mathcal{X}$ $\mathcal{X}$ $\mathcal{X}$

$\mathcal{X}$ $\mathcal{X}$ $\mathcal{X}$ $\mathcal{X}$ $\mathcal{X}$ $\mathcal{X}$ $\mathcal{X}$ $\mathcal{X}$ $\mathcal{X}$ $\mathcal{X}$ $\mathcal{X}$ $\mathcal{X}$ $\mathcal{X}$ $\mathcal{X}$ $\mathcal{X}$

$\mathcal{X}$ $\mathcal{X}$ $\mathcal{X}$ $\mathcal{X}$ $\mathcal{X}$ $\mathcal{X}$ $\mathcal{X}$ $\mathcal{X}$ $\mathcal{X}$ $\mathcal{X}$ $\mathcal{X}$ $\mathcal{X}$ $\mathcal{X}$ $\mathcal{X}$ $\mathcal{X}$

$\mathcal{X}$ $\mathcal{X}$ $\mathcal{X}$ $\mathcal{X}$ $\mathcal{X}$ $\mathcal{X}$ $\mathcal{X}$ $\mathcal{X}$ $\mathcal{X}$ $\mathcal{X}$ $\mathcal{X}$ $\mathcal{X}$ $\mathcal{X}$ $\mathcal{X}$ $\mathcal{X}$

$\mathcal{X}$ $\mathcal{X}$ $\mathcal{X}$ $\mathcal{X}$ $\mathcal{X}$ $\mathcal{X}$ $\mathcal{X}$ $\mathcal{X}$ $\mathcal{X}$ $\mathcal{X}$ $\mathcal{X}$ $\mathcal{X}$ $\mathcal{X}$ $\mathcal{X}$ $\mathcal{X}$

x x x x x x x x x x x x x x

x x x x x x x x x x x x x x

x x x x x x x x x x x x x x

x x x x x x x x x x x x x x

x x x x x x x x x x x x x x

Trace the letter Xx. Then write the letter Xx as many times as possible.

$\mathcal{X}\, x \quad Xanthium$

$\mathcal{X} \;\; \mathcal{X} \;\; \mathcal{X}$

$\mathcal{X} \;\; \mathcal{X} \;\; \mathcal{X}$

$\mathcal{X} \;\; \mathcal{X} \;\; \mathcal{X}$

$\mathcal{X} \;\; \mathcal{X} \;\; \mathcal{X}$

$\mathcal{X} \;\; \mathcal{X} \;\; \mathcal{X}$

$\mathcal{X} \;\; \mathcal{X} \;\; \mathcal{X}$

$x \;\; x \;\; x \;\; x$

$x \;\; x \;\; x \;\; x$

$x \;\; x \;\; x \;\; x$

$x \;\; x \;\; x \;\; x$

$x \;\; x \;\; x \;\; x$

Write the sentence onto the lines below. Then trace and write the letters.

X was King Xerxes,

Who wore on his head

A mighty large turban,

Green, yellow, and red.

X X X

X X X

x x x

x x x

Trace the letter Yy.

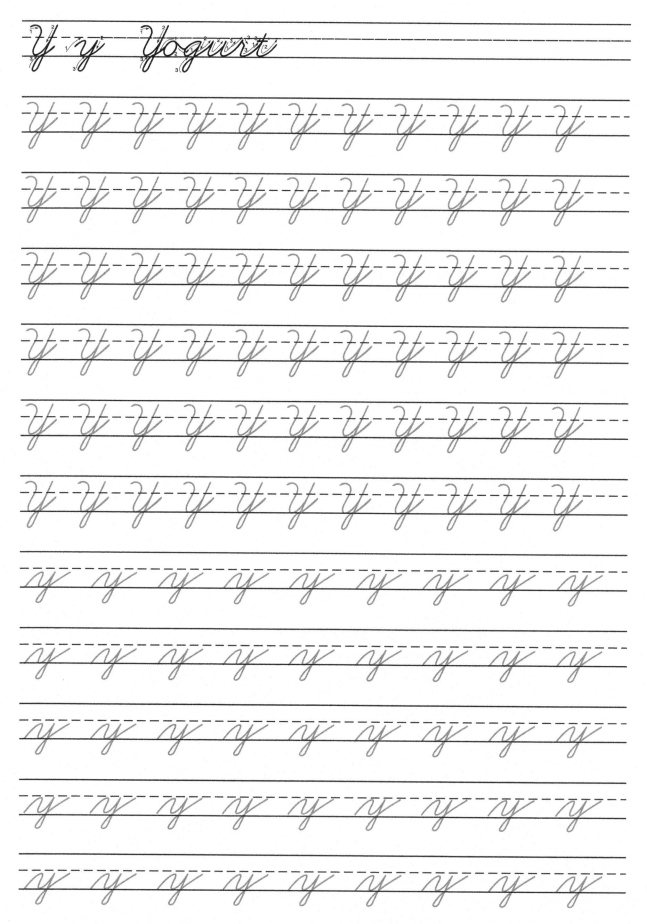

Learn to Write in Cursive: Handwriting Practice Workbook

Trace the letter Yy.

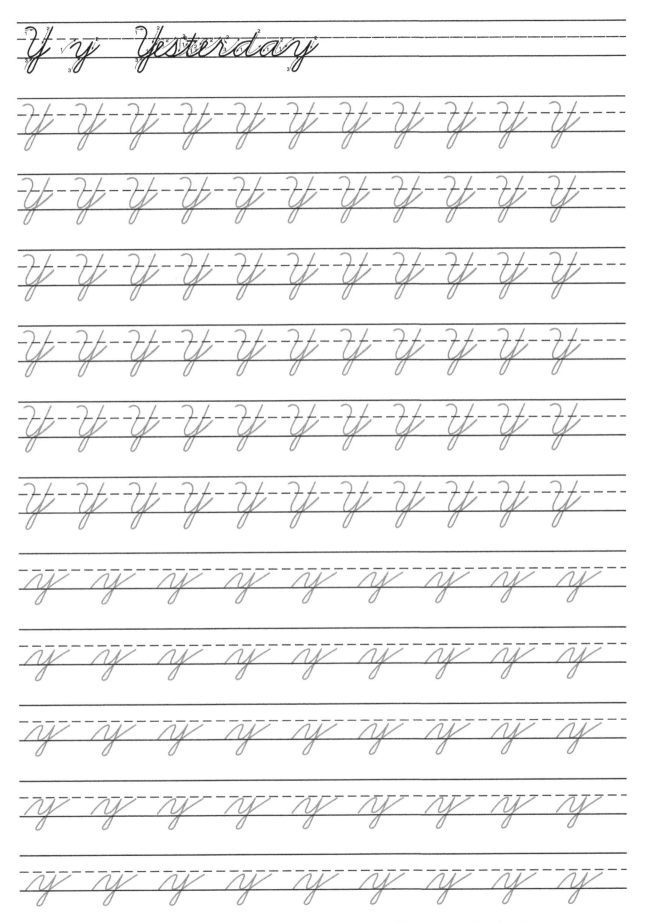

Trace the letter Yy. Then write the letter Yy as many times as possible.

$\mathcal{Y}\,y\qquad\mathcal{Y}east$

$\mathcal{Y}\quad\mathcal{Y}\quad\mathcal{Y}$

$\mathcal{Y}\quad\mathcal{Y}\quad\mathcal{Y}$

$\mathcal{Y}\quad\mathcal{Y}\quad\mathcal{Y}$

$\mathcal{Y}\quad\mathcal{Y}\quad\mathcal{Y}$

$\mathcal{Y}\quad\mathcal{Y}\quad\mathcal{Y}$

$\mathcal{Y}\quad\mathcal{Y}\quad\mathcal{Y}$

$y\quad y\quad y$

$y\quad y\quad y$

$y\quad y\quad y$

$y\quad y\quad y$

$y\quad y\quad y$

Learn to Write in Cursive: Handwriting Practice Workbook

Write the sentence onto the lines below. Then trace and write the letters.

Y was a yak,

From the land of Thibet.

Except his white tail,

He was all black as jet.

Y Y Y

Y Y Y

Y Y Y

Y Y Y

Trace the letter Zz.

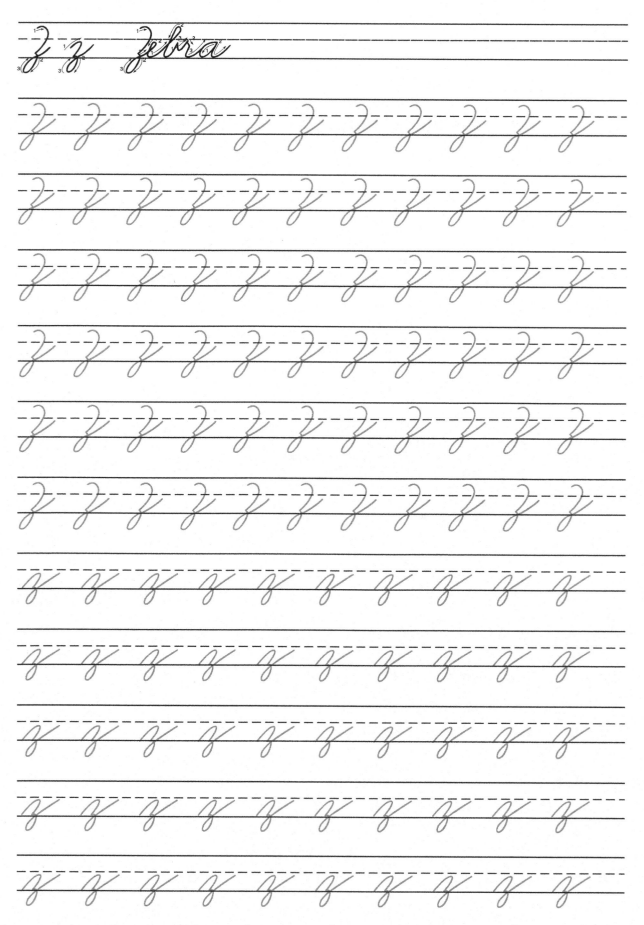

Learn to Write in Cursive: Handwriting Practice Workbook

Trace the letter Zz.

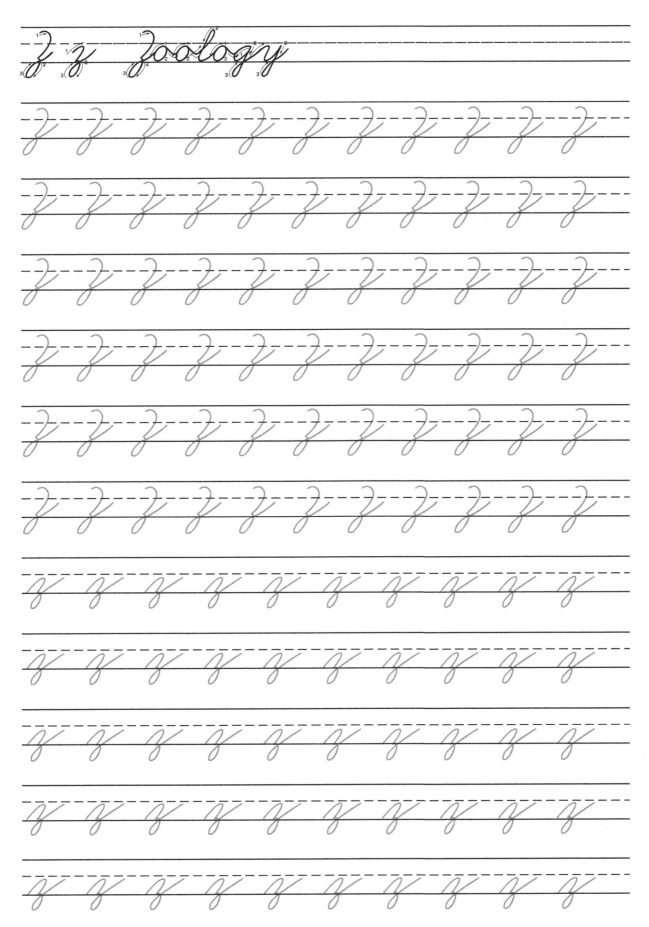

Trace the letter Zz. Then write the letter Zz as many times as possible.

Z z Ziplock

Learn to Write in Cursive: Handwriting Practice Workbook

Write the sentence onto the lines below. Then trace and write the letters.

Z was a zebra,

Striped white and black;

And if he were tame,

You might ride on his back.

Z Z Z

Z Z Z

Z Z Z

Z Z Z

Learn to Write in Cursive: Handwriting Practice Workbook

Made in the USA
Monee, IL
03 July 2020